Have a B

Contents

Have a Ball

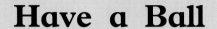

If you have a ball,
you can play a game!
You can play on your
own or with friends.
You can throw balls.
You can bounce them.
You can kick balls,
or hit them with a bat.

Head It

Soccer is played with a round ball. There are eleven players on a soccer team.

Players move the ball down the field with their feet. To score a goal, they kick the ball or hit it with their head. Only the goalkeeper is allowed to catch the ball.

4

Object of the Game

To get the ball into the other team's net and score a goal.

5

Hit It

Baseball is played with a bat and a small, hard ball. There are nine players on a team.

The pitcher throws the ball to the batter. The batter has three chances to hit the ball. Once three players are "out," the other side goes up to bat.

6

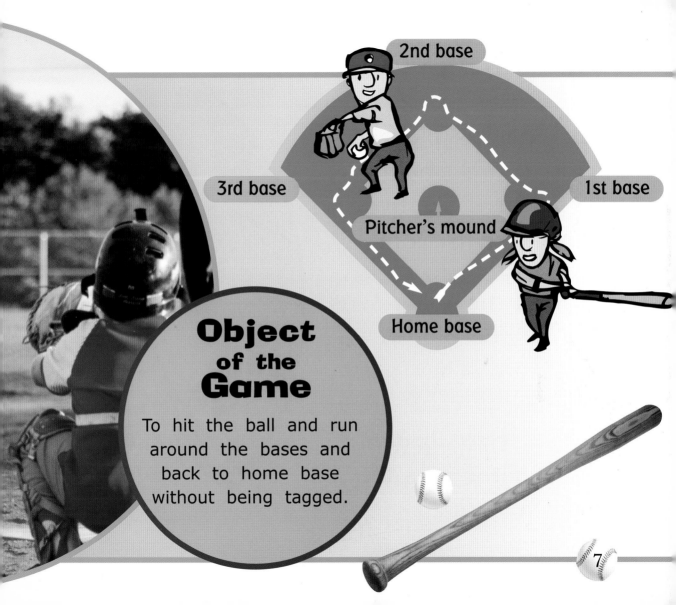

2nd base

3rd base

1st base

Pitcher's mound

Home base

Object of the Game

To hit the ball and run around the bases and back to home base without being tagged.

7

Dunk It

Basketball is played with a large, bouncy ball. There are five players on a team.

Players run and bounce the ball down the court. They pass the ball to each other. They try to shoot it through the hoop to score a basket.

Object
of the
Game

To score points, players must shoot the ball through the hoop, or basket, at the end of the court.

9

Smash It

Tennis players use a racket to hit a small ball over a net to the player on the other side. There can be two or four players in a tennis game.

The ball is only allowed to bounce once before it must be hit back over the net.

Object
of the
Game

To hit the ball over the net within the court area. If a player on the other side is unable to return the ball, a point is scored.

Spike It

Volleyball is played with a ball and net. There are up to six players on a volleyball team. Players use their hands to hit a large, light ball over the net.

Volleyball can be played inside or outside. It can even be played in a swimming pool!

Object
of the
Game

To hit the ball over the net within the court area. If a player on the other side is unable to hit the ball back before it touches the ground, a point is scored.

Whack It

Croquet is played with sticks called mallets, and hard, colored balls.

Players try to knock their ball through wickets that are set up on the court. A player can knock another player's ball off the court with their ball.

Object
of the
Game

To go through all the wickets and be the first player to reach and hit the stake, which is set up in the center of the court.

Throw It

Bocce is played with small, heavy balls. An even smaller ball called the jack is thrown onto the court.

Players throw their balls, trying to place them close to the jack. Players also try to knock other balls away from the jack.

Object
of the
Game

When all the balls have been thrown, the winning ball is the one closest to the jack.

Sink It

Golf is played with clubs and a small ball. It is played on a golf course with eighteen holes.

Players hit their ball around the course. They must hit their ball into each hole. Players count the number of strokes they take to get around the course.

Object
of the
Game

To get around the eighteen holes with the least number of shots.

Bowl It

Bowling is played indoors at a bowling alley. Players bowl a large, heavy ball at pins standing at the end of the alley.

Players try to knock down as many pins as they can in two tries.

Object
of the
Game

The player who has knocked down the most pins at the end of the game is the winner.

Try This!

Four Square

What you need:
- Four people.
- A large, bouncy ball.
- A court marked out in four squares— one square marked with START.

START

How to play the game:

1 Each player stands
   in a square.
2 The player in the START square
   pat-bounces the ball to
   another player who pats
   it to another player.
3 The ball is only allowed
   to bounce once
   in a player's square.

Index